SUPERNATURAL PROVISION

Learning to Walk in Greater Levels of Stewardship and
Responsibility and Letting Go of Unbiblical Beliefs

MICHAEL VAN VLYMEN

Copyright © 2018 Michael Van Vlymen

MINISTRY RESOURCES

All rights reserved. No part of this publication may be reproduced, distributed, or transmitted in any form or by any means, including photocopying, recording, or other electronic or mechanical methods, without the prior written permission of the publisher, except in the case of brief quotations embodied in critical reviews and certain other noncommercial uses permitted by copyright law.

ISBN – 13: 978-1-948680-00-4
ISBN- 10: 1-948680-00-9

DEDICATION

I would like to dedicate this book to a few people. First to my parents, Marvin and Cathy who taught their children to be generous and kind and gave us "lessons" in sharing whether we liked it or not. Then to my wife Gordana who really understood more than I that all of the blessings God has given us are His to direct through us as stewards. And to the Lord Jesus Christ who has shown Himself faithful so many times that He makes it easy to believe Him with all things... even our provision.

CONTENTS

	Introduction	i
1	Are We Walking in Supernatural Provision?	1
2	Traditions and Mindsets	9
3	Church vs. Kingdom	19
4	Popular Teachings	35
5	Wisdom Concerning Spiritual Things	51
6	Setting Things Right	57
	About the Author	

INTRODUCTION

In this book Supernatural Provision I hope to challenge you. I hope to get you to really think through some of the things we do and learn to undo them. I'm going to ask you to rethink everything and then re-evaluate using scripture as a plumb-line along with the Holy Spirit as the one who reveals the truth of those scriptures. This first book is a wakeup call.

The second book of this series is an examination of the most basic things we are doing with our money, how the Lord expects us to behave with our finances and using faith to see the promises of God come to pass. The second book is a book of steps of faith and action in our stewardship as well as testimonies of miracles of provision.

I hope you will pray on these things and begin to walk in great measures of Supernatural Provision.

1

Are We Walking in Supernatural Provision?

Recently I posted something on Facebook where I basically asked this question. If believers can heal the sick, raise the dead, cast out devils, work miracles etc., then why does this power we carry not seem to work with too many people concerning their finances? I asked the question... Does this seem odd to anyone. There was a mixed bag of answers. To many it did seem odd and to others it was normal.

Can I share what goes through my mind when I think about this scenario? It's like Superman asking for bus fare. You would wonder... Hey! You are Superman! Just take off those glasses and tie and fly where you need to go. Bus fare Superman? Come on!

Think about this in the average Christian home. We have the promises of God, and we know He does not lie, so that is not even a question, which means we are not in unbelief or doubt about His promises of provision. Yet how many families are constantly trying to get to that place where they are not stressed out concerning how to pay bills or provide little extras for their kids or family?

Think about this in the realm of ministry for a minute. We feel called to go to a church or a region and see the power of God on display to change people's lives. We tell the Pastor to expect to see miracles!. Expect to see healings! Expect to see demonstrations of God's power! God is telling us to go! Now ... If we can only raise enough money for gas to get there. If that does not seem strange to you then I'm not explaining this right!

The supernatural should not stop at your wallet or bank account. That is my opinion. I'm probably going to say some things that will be offensive to some people. I know I'm going to say some things that many will not agree with. Let's see if there are some other things that don't quite line up.

What Does the Word Say?

There are many scriptures that talk about blessing and increase. There are promises and admonitions, instructions and covenants. God has already given provision has He not? Seek the Kingdom of God above all else, and he will give you everything you need. Luke 12:31

And my God will fully supply your every need according to his glorious riches in the Messiah Jesus. Philippians 4:19
So if you sinful people know how to give good gifts to your children, how much more will your heavenly Father give good gifts to those who ask him. Matthew 7:11

Therefore I tell you, whatever you ask for in prayer, believe that you have received it, and it will be yours. Mark 11:24

For it was I, the LORD your God, who rescued you from the land of Egypt. Open your mouth wide, and I will fill it with good things. Psalm 81:10

Provisionally, these things are already given in the Word. You say no Mike He has really given it. Yes... I know that, but what I am talking about is have you received it? Many say "Yes, I have received it by faith." That is still not what I'm talking about. Have you received it so that you can literally carry it to the store and buy groceries? Or pay bills? Or ....?

It is not doubt and unbelief to say that something has not yet manifested in the natural realm. My point is.... Are you walking in supernatural provision right now so that if someone were to look at your life, they would wonder what makes you so blessed?

Well Mike, it's not all about having new cars and a big house and fancy clothes so that we can show off. Yes we shouldn't be in pride about anything the Father has given us, that's true. But it isn't wrong or ungodly to have a nice car. If missionaries were to come through town and you wanted to loan your car to them for the week, could you say that they would have something nice and reliable to drive, or would you be worried about it breaking down?

Let's say you don't want or need a big house. That's fine. How about being blessed and actually walking in it so that the people who look at your life would see you always traveling to here and there, putting in water wells for villages or providing other needs across the world or across your neighborhood.

Well... it's not about what others see, some might say. Yes it is. That is part of it. The Word talks about this.

In the same way, let your light shine before others, that they may see your good deeds and glorify your Father in heaven. (Matthew 5:16 NIV)

Are you really walking in divine provision? What is it about our lives that would cause people to look at you and say God has really given them favor? Or what is it about your life that says your God is the true God?

There are many right now who are reading these words and are already arguing in their own minds with the words I've written. I know that. I see resistance to this when speaking face to face with people so I expect it will be here also.

It is usually one of two things that people have a problem with. One, when believers speak of financial blessing, to many that means having money to consumes upon their own lusts. "She doesn't need a nicer car! She's a woman of God!" "Why do they have to be dressed that way?! This isn't Hollywood!"

And two, many have the idea that they have received God's blessing by faith and now they just wait for God's timing and it will be manifested according to His timing and His will. This sounds almost Biblical and humble and holy but this doesn't "fly" in the real world, yet we put our eggs in this basket when it comes to provision. What do I mean?

If you are praying for a loved one who is sick to receive healing, do you pray once, receive it by faith and then wait to see it manifested? I sure hope not. If you need a job, do you pray about it, receive one by faith and then wait and watch? If that were true there would be many more with unpaid bills and kids going hungry.

The idea that we should "go after" provision that God has given us sounds offensive to so many and as I said it is because of a wrong mindset about what that means.

I was talking to a friend recently about these topics and in the midst of our conversation, he said, or declared the scriptures as an answer to my question. He said " I am blessed in the city and I am blessed in the country, I am blessed going in and blessed coming out.... Etc." (According to Deuteronomy 28:3) (and I believe in this)

I said to him, you are not walking in that. He got offended and told me he was. I said you just got through telling me earlier that your kids had needs and you don't have the money for it. He got angry with me.

As I said, it is not doubt and unbelief to acknowledge that something has not yet manifested in the natural realm that has already been given by Heaven.

Why Is This Provision Issue so Important?

A big answer is because people have needs. One of the ways the enemy sows strife is by afflicting people's finances. I just heard in my spirit someone else arguing about this statement. So... Let me say that what I am writing here is for those who are NOT currently walking in supernatural provision the way they would like to. All of you who already have the answers, God bless you! That's great! I'm talking to those who may have needs.

A friend of mine was telling me recently about an acquaintance at church who is constantly making the declarations about financial blessing over himself. He claims that he follows the voice of the Spirit and that God always provides. Sounds good right? He gives away money to many people for many seemingly absurd reasons. (God told me to buy everyone in the church WWJD wristbands) Still... what is the harm there? The problem here is an ongoing one in that he never has money to actually pay his bills or take care of financial obligations.

He said that this young man then lets everyone know he has no money for rent but God will provide. Of course, many feel sorry for this eager young man and give him money for his bills. It is a vicious cycle with him and a poor testimony.

If we are making declarations about how good God is and "living by faith" yet constantly have to borrow money to meet the bills, it's time to learn something about supernatural provision. If you are trying to lead your friends or family to Christ yet constantly have to come to them, the unbelievers for money, it causes a reason for them not to believe.

Let me tell you a testimony friend shared with me.

My friend said that they had been preaching the Gospel for

many years in an indian tribe in the jungle. They had less than a handful of converts to show for years of diligent work with this tribe. Then God did something spectacular! He baptized them in the Holy Spirit! So after that happened they began doing the greater works along with preaching the Gospel. Suddenly they were healing the sick and dealing with other issues in the power of God. Can you guess what happened? In one year they went from less than ten believers to several hundred! What was the difference?

Those in the tribe said that they reasoned why should we accept this new God that can't help us in any way? They liked the story of the Gospel but had not seen the manifestation of it's power.

For many reasons I believe we must walk in supernatural provision. Don't entertain all the reasons why we shouldn't. Step back for a moment and think of all the reasons why we should. Allow the Holy Spirit to show you greater revelation about Kingdom Finances.

Why I Feel Compelled to Share with You

I have kind of wrestled with this a little bit, about whether to share on this subject. God has been teaching us about the provision of Heaven for a while now and has given us many lessons in that area. But, I know that there have been so many abuses in this area it makes me more than hesitant to speak on it. You know what I'm talking about and I will get into that a bit more very soon.

I have seen people in ministry do the most ungodly things when it comes to money and I told the Lord that I never, ever want to be a part of that. Ever..

Yet... The Lord has taught us about this subject and given us supernatural experiences in finances. How does that work Lord? I want to share about this but not be somehow lumped together with those who have ulterior motives for teaching on this subject.

Can I just throw in a disclaimer here and say that I have many friends who teach on this subject and have written solid revelation on supernatural provision that are Kingdom minded people. It's the classic wheat and tares issue.

Heavens Bounty Manifested

I don't know of any gentle way to say this, so I'll just say it. God has blessed us. It hasn't been an easy journey by any stretch of the imagination because we had lessons to learn and years of ungodly mindsets to be set free from where money was concerned.

But God has shown us that SUPERNATURAL provision is available. That in itself is a key. What exactly do I mean by that. Well... those who know me know that I tell all as much as I feel the Lord allows and He allows a lot!

I will share more about this this, but let me just say that angels have literally put money into my hand. What??? Yes. And I am not talking ..."well.. I felt that God was putting something in my hand.." No, I mean literal, physical money.
I was speaking once in a conference, and telling many testimonies of angelic visitations and the supernatural, but when I mentioned about angels giving me money, you could have heard a pin drop. Do you know what that tells me? People have needs to be met and want to know!

God has literally multiplied money for us, the most recent time that comes to mind was a month ago.

You may be wondering "how much money?" Some of you would be impressed and others would not. I will share more about this.

The Lord has given us "lessons" and experiences in financial provision. I'm going to share it with you. I pray it helps and blesses you and encourages you. I believe that this is part of my work so please know my heart, that there is no ulterior motive in me (that I am aware of) thus my reluctance to share in the first place.

I never want to be one of those guys who whose only message seems to be "make me a cake" and make sure it's a big cake and put it in the mail today. I hope I made myself clear on this one. ☐ I still love and pray for those guys just so you know.

But I pray that as I share some of the revelation that God has given me with you, that you would prayerfully consider the words I write and see what the Lord tells you.

2

Traditions and Mindsets

I could just write a simple list... I think you should do x, y and z. But that is what I feel we should not do. An instruction like that should have no "teeth." Many people who talk about finances, sowing, and prosperity today, want you to just do what they tell you to do because they are experts. They have written books on the subject or they are on TV, or a combination. Many have heard from the Lord. Well... I have heard from the Lord on this subject and have been taught many lessons about supernatural prosperity. But I don't want you to do what I say just because I had a revelation, I want you to prayerfully consider the things I say and ask the Lord to give you an inner witness and confirm these things to you. I will spill the beans a bit. We are in the trouble we are in because we don't see what the Father is doing before we act. So as you read my words, "look" and see what the Father is doing.

Traditions of men are either non-godly or ungodly things we may do that are either accepted as "godly" by believers both religious and non-religious, or are tolerated by us, or are things we do by rote, not thinking about them as we do them. Some are not in and of themselves ungodly, but when we do them against God's will, our act then is ungodly. It is not profitable to prefer the traditions of men over the Word of God, in any way, about anything. When we talk about the

Gospel and the power of the Gospel, it becomes real obvious to most of us why we should reject the traditions of men. Real obvious? OK... Maybe not real obvious.

Several years ago, I was watching a television program that is hosted by a Jewish believer who teaches on the heritage and practice, rituals and clothing, etc., of Jewish worship and how that should be brought into practice by believers today, and how this brings an added element to our Christian walk. He gave all of the Biblical evidences and reasons, citing several passages in the Old Testament, and I was blown away. I got so excited by his message I couldn't wait to order some of the items he was selling. After the program, I literally ran upstairs to tell my wife. I was going to take her through the same Old Testament passage he had talked about. I knew she would be excited too! When I opened my mouth to speak and tell her the passage, something else came out of my mouth. I said "Gordana! You have to hear this! We have to read Galatians 5!"

When I heard the words that came out of my mouth, I was confused. Actually, I was very confused for a moment, and I realized that the Lord was telling me to read Galatians chapter 5. Although I didn't remember that passage at the time, I sure can't forget it now.

Stand fast therefore in the liberty by which Christ has made us free,[a] and do not be entangled again with a yoke of bondage. 2 Indeed I, Paul, say to you that if you become circumcised, Christ will profit you nothing. 3 And I testify again to every man who becomes circumcised that he is a debtor to keep the whole law. 4 You have become estranged from Christ, you who attempt to be justified by law; you have fallen from grace. 5 For we through the Spirit eagerly wait for the hope of righteousness by faith. 6 For in Christ Jesus neither circumcision nor uncircumcision avails anything, but faith working through love. (Galatians 5:1-6 KJV) (read the whole chapter)

Here Paul is telling believers not to get sucked back in to following traditions because it makes the Gospel of no effect. With everything that God has shown me, I would have thought that I would have realized that, but that whole tradition thing just sounded so right. The Lord actually put words in my own mouth to correct me. I am not saying don't honor the feast days or anything like that. What I am saying is, I heard something and it sounded good, so I was going to do it. I didn't ask the Lord about it. It was not revelation to me, it was some religious things I thought I could do to enhance my Christian walk.

My point here is that this tradition was not even something that I had been raised in, or even exposed to, yet still it drew me. Plus, the words of a man caused me to want to do something without even thinking or praying about it. My point is that the teaching sounded so good and so biblical and wise, it moved me to act apart from the revelation of God.

The fact that so "many believers are discovering and celebrating their roots" was a draw to me also. Everybody else is doing it. The crowd mentality should not be a part of us either. We are to be led of the Spirit.

For as many as are led by the Spirit of God, they are the sons of God. (Romans 8:14 KJV)

More about Traditions

More about traditions? I want to know about supernatural provision! Yes, I get that. I'm getting there but this plays a role in why we are not walking in abundance and overflow.

We do things all year long that are questionable at best. We do things that have no basis in Scripture and we accept them. I don't want this to be about holidays, but that is an obvious example and it plays a part in the grand scheme. Years ago when I heard certain ministers begin to talk about the origins of "Christian" holidays, I thought, here is another one of those nuts that takes everything too far and makes believers look like a bunch of over reactive isolationists. I mean... what harm is it really? Santa Claus... so what? The Easter bunny? I'm not celebrating the Easter bunny. I mean, yes, we hide eggs and give chocolate bunnies and all that but it's not like it means something to us. Christmas? Yes, I understand the origin of the tree and the gifts and the melding of the beliefs of the pagans and the Christians, but I don't worship the tree and I do believe in Jesus. Yes... I do spend too much money at Christmas time but it's only once a year. Etc., etc. And on and on it goes. This is not about whether you give Christmas gifts or say merry Christmas. I am hoping I can show you and you will see the bigger picture.

My point is that we do the things we do, not because we are compelled by God or the scripture or even some inner witness or conviction that "this is the right thing to do" but because of "this is what I know, and this is the way we have always done it." (Are you thinking money yet?)

In my house, I declare over my family the things that I believe are vital to us because I know they are of God, and it really doesn't matter to me whether anyone else is on board or not. Do you have things like that in your life? For me, one of them would be "as for me and my house we will serve the Lord." To me that is non-negotiable and etched in stone. But in the framework of what I have mentioned, I would not be able to say "as for me and my house, we will celebrate_____." (pick any holiday) There is no conviction there. If we do celebrate something it is only because we are maintaining the status quo. We have always done it this way.

I hope that you are not thinking that all this is about wasting money on holidays, because it's not. There is a much bigger picture. The bigger point being, we make decisions about much of life by just maintaining the status quo. It is decision by default. This includes our finances. Our decision is that we just keep doing the same thing over and over, waiting for the blessings to roll in. "What should we do? Let's increase the amount because maybe that's why we haven't seen any fruit yet. It must be us....let's sow more." Why do we believe what we believe? Have we studied and prayed? Have we fasted over our money issues? Are we just listening to bunch of ideas or instructions that sound good or sound right? It must be right because that is what everyone else believes and does. Are we hearing God's voice or just doing what we have always done?

We have heard and followed instructions for so long it's like we are asleep at the wheel. We end up somewhere and don't even know how we got there. When we discover we still haven't gotten the breakthrough we just know it has to be our fault. Or... our spouse. "What have you done to destroy our blessing? Are you in some secret sin?"

My wife Gordana and I used to go to conferences all the time, where we knew the power and the anointing of God would be present and tangible. We always went in the hope and the belief that we would receive some life changing touch or blessing of some kind. If Benny Hinn had a meeting within 500 miles of our house, we would be there. I remember one trip to Chicago when he was speaking at the United Center and we loaded up the whole family and went. We prayed and sang and worshipped on the way there, preparing our hearts and just knowing that this time would be one that would be life-changing.

It was probably the 20th meeting of his we had been to. It was glorious. It was anointed and encouraging and more! But, on the way home we were talking about the meeting. "Do you really feel that it was life-changing this time?" I asked Gordana. "No .:she said. "It was so good but not life-changing." So from that point, our conversation kind of went downhill a bit. Suddenly we are having a mild argument over whose fault it was we didn't get the breakthrough. By then my wife was looking at me suspiciously. "Is there something you want to tell me?" "No." "Do you even want a breakthrough?" "Yes., of course!" "Were you in faith?" Yes I certainly was." It had to be something, so assuming the problem was with me she kept asking. "Did you sow?" "Yes I did." "Did you sow the twenty dollars you had?" "Uh, no. I sowed fifteen.' "I knew it was you! You ruined our breakthrough!"

In hindsight it may be just a little funny now, but back then we had this conversation way too many times. Whether we were talking about breakthrough in finances or breakthrough in spiritual things, we didn't feel that we were receiving what the Word said we could expect, and we couldn't really see what, if anything, we were doing wrong. And so we continued on year after year, doing what we had always done because that is what we knew. Sure, we tried it with more faith, or more money, or more prayer, or more desire, but in the end we were not seeing increase of biblical proportions.

What does the Bible say?

Give, and it shall be given unto you; good measure, pressed down, and shaken together, and running over, shall men give into your bosom. For with the same measure that ye mete withal it shall be measured to you again. (Luke 6:38 KJV)

Traditions... whether formal, informal or subconscious, doing things without really thinking about it or weighing the consequences of our actions, believing everything is OK. I know you have heard the definition of insanity given like this...

"Insanity: Doing the same thing over and over and expecting a different result."

Mindsets

A mindset is a mental attitude or inclination or a fixed state of mind. Mindset is further defined as a fixed mental attitude or disposition that predetermines a person's responses to and interpretations of situations. An inclination or a habit, according to Merriam-Webster and the Free Dictionary. This is a fairly accurate definition. I would also add, that it is a framework of support through which our thought processes function and direct us. I realized that after I had some experiences in the spiritual realm however. It wasn't readily apparent to me previous to that. (the framework)

We know that almost without exception, the way we think and believe is set in our childhood, and apart from the intervention of God, most people don't deviate from that. We watch and learn at home. What brings us reward and what brings punishment. We take in everything mostly because we have no ability to reason. Reason being to make correct choices by comparing things against knowledge and life experience which as children we have nothing apart from those who have taught us.

Why am I going here to talk about supernatural provision? Because a lot of what we believe and do is not from God, yet we expect Him to perform as though it were. Please don't get defensive... not this early anyway. As the Lord was teaching me about the framework around our beliefs, I was thinking about all of the things I have learned about sowing and reaping and godly stewardship and things of that nature.

I realized that the people who helped to build my belief system about money and these issues of biblical understanding of money, are the same people who taught me God doesn't heal anymore or deliver people from demons or perform miracles etc. If all the things they taught me about those issues were wrong, why would I blindly continue to believe what they taught me about sowing and reaping etc.? It never occurred to me until the Lord began to show us some things.

From the time we are born, we are exposed to this world's system. It is all around us and directs the way the world believes and acts. From school to television to generation upon generation we perform in line with those around us. Not you? Ok. Maybe not. How do you define success? What are the evidences of success? What are the dreams you have for your children? Is it vastly different from the rest of the world? How we dress, how we behave, which careers are "worthy" and which are "low", how we feel about people who have a lot or a little are all things we have generally been taught.

We in general have always tried to solve our own problems and money issues by natural means, planning, saving and investing. Nothing wrong with being a good steward by the way. I am not throwing rocks at you, Many times I have been the guy who has said "well, we've done all we can do, let's pray." Why is prayer always the last resort? It should be the very first thing we do. There is a framework of the world around us, that constantly reinforces the ideals it has about money, and prosperity, and provision.
Yes, even in the church! We have been taught principles that have been handed down from generation to generation.

Interpretations of scriptures are given to us by people we know love God, so we assume they are correct. Don't believe it?

Never is this desire to think and reason and react according to the world more evident than it is when Christians start talking about politics. Even though we are espousing "godly virtues" we are doing it from the ground. It is shameful sometimes, but definitely disappointing to me that believers come down from their place of Heavenly authority to roll around in the gutter like mere men when it comes to politics, and many other things for that matter. Do you remember the angel who spoke to Joshua?

13. Now when Joshua was near Jericho, he looked up and saw a man standing in front of him with a drawn sword in his hand. Joshua went up to him and asked, "Are you for us or for our enemies?"

14 "Neither," he replied, "but as commander of the army of the Lord I have now come." Then Joshua fell facedown to the ground in reverence, and asked him, "What message does my Lord[a] have for his servant?" (Joshua 5:13, 14 NIV)

Do you know who we are supposed to be like? Joshua figured it out quickly. We need to be like Joshua. We must stop looking at ourselves as participants of this worlds system even when it comes to unbiblical church teachings and culture. We have to ask the Lord, "Lord, what do you say? What message does my Lord have for His servant?"

If we are going to walk in supernatural provision, we have to make room to let God be God. He has to rule and reign in our lives. There has to come a shift where we ask the Lord to bring understanding about who we really are and we have to be willing to be that person. Many are to afraid to even consider these things. The fear of punishment seems to be a greater motivator than the possibility of reward. We don't have a clue what God has prepared for us. We cannot think or imagine at that level. Even in dreams or visions it is hard to grasp the splendor of His glory and His Kingdom. It's His good pleasure to give you the Kingdom you know?

Fear not, little flock; for it is your Father's good pleasure to give you the kingdom. (Luke 12:32 KJV)

If we are going to walk in supernatural provision, we have to embrace the Kingdom and live from a different place. If we will do that, it makes room for the abundance of Heaven to flow.

3

Church vs Kingdom

The Early Church

The early church was the ecclesia. This is the Greek word translated "church" in our Bibles. The meaning of ecclesia as opposed to what "church" has become to mean today is vastly different. The ecclesia are those who are called out, those who gather together for a purpose. In the Kingdom, ecclesia would be those who are called out of this world and unto God. We are called out of this world's system. In Matthew chapter five it tells us...

3 "Let me tell you why you are here. You're here to be salt-seasoning that brings out the God-flavors of this earth. If you lose your saltiness, how will people taste godliness? You've lost your usefulness and will end up in the garbage.

14-16 "Here's another way to put it: You're here to be light, bringing out the God-colors in the world. God is not a secret to be kept. We're going public with this, as public as a city on a hill. If I make you light-bearers, you don't think I'm going to hide you under a bucket, do you? I'm putting you on a light stand. Now that I've put you there on a hilltop, on a light stand—shine! Keep open house; be generous with your lives. By opening up to others, you'll prompt people to open up with God, this generous Father in heaven. (Matthew 5:13-16 NKJV)

16 So from now on we regard no one from a worldly point of view. Though we once regarded Christ in this way, we do so no longer. 17 Therefore, if anyone is in Christ, the new creation has come:[a] The old has gone, the new is here! 18 All this is from God, who reconciled us to himself through Christ and gave us the ministry of reconciliation: 19 that God was reconciling the world to himself in Christ, not counting people's sins against them. And he has committed to us the message of reconciliation. 20 We are therefore Christ's ambassadors, as though God were making his appeal through us. We implore you on Christ's behalf: Be reconciled to God. 21 God made him who had no sin to be sin[b] for us, so that in him we might become the righteousness of God. (2 Corinthians 16-21 NIV)

We are reconciled to God through Christ. We as the ecclesia are new creation beings who do not see things as those in the world see them. The Bible also says that we are called out of darkness...

But ye are a chosen generation, a royal priesthood, an holy nation, a peculiar people; that ye should shew forth the praises of him who hath called you out of darkness into his marvellous light: (1 Peter 2:9 KJV)

People who live in darkness do not see things clearly, they make bad decisions for much of life because of that. We who are called out, the ecclesia, not only are in the light but also bear the light to lead others into relationship with Christ. We see things that others do not see. The Bible tells us that we are seated in Heavenly places in Christ. This is a standing of authority in the spirit realm, and in all realms actually that gives us a vantage point from God's perspective. Seeing from God's perspective gives us wisdom and revelation to move in and navigate every realm and situation.

This is the way we are supposed to function. This relates to the first analogy I gave about Superman. We are so far beyond what the world understands, it would be unbelievable if we had not experienced it for ourselves.

This was what the early church had... a called out existence, moving in supernatural power as sons of God, doing the works of Christ for the glory of God. This is to be our normal. When I share through my books and with congregations that everyone can see in the spirit, move in heavenly realms and interact daily with angels, it is not just flowery, encouraging speech. This is the reality of who we are supposed to be, and what we are supposed to walk in. Many times just acknowledging this gives people the breakthrough that they need to live in it. The more we gain understanding of who we really are in Christ the greater the manifestation of the Kingdom of Heaven in us and through us.

The early church met together in people's homes, many times secretly because of the persecution of the church (ecclesia). Many times the fellowship or gathering together would include meals where people might pitch in and contribute. When those surrounding their lives had needs, the ecclesia gave to help them. (Understand here I am referring to the called out ones and not the organization or church building) When people "brought their money into the storehouse" what did that mean?

Bring the whole tithe into the storehouse, that there may be food in my house. Test me in this," says the LORD Almighty, "and see if I will not throw open the floodgates of heaven and pour out so much blessing that there will not be room enough to store it. (Malachi 3:10 NIV)

If there were a group of say ten or twenty believers gathering as the called out ones in someone's home to worship and glorify God, and be built up by teaching and fellowship, what exactly would the "storehouse" be? Was it some special place that they all sent their money to? No, for the new covenant believers it was not following a rule as if under the law, but was an operation of the sons of God (daughters included of course) to do what God does. Using God's money to help and care for people, showing people that God cares by their actions. I can imagine they picked someone to hold the funds and when they saw needs they moved as God spoke to them.

What about family with needs? Would this also count? Let's say that one of these twenty people had a distant aunt who was recently widowed and needed help. Would this woman be disqualified from that help because she is a relative? Could you use the money set aside for God's work to help her or would they have to take a vote on it because of the family connection. Do you see what I'm doing here? I am introducing the way the modern "church" thinks about God's money and the storehouse. No, of course they would help her. It isn't even a question for those called out ones. What about closer family connections? Does it get a little muddier? No it does not. We are called to do the works of God in this Earth, and listen to and obey His voice. It is as simple as that. What if God spoke to one person and told them to help someone? Would they have to take a vote before they obey God, or could they just obey God?

It doesn't seem that simple for most of us because we have been taught that certain passages of scripture mean certain things, not according to scripture, but our understanding of scripture reinforced by centuries of tradition and church protocol. These things are passed down from generation to the next and carry the weight of tradition which is a very powerful thing. It is hard for people to go against tradition. For most it would be easier to go against the Word of God.

Right now people are weighing whether to believe this. I get it. I would not believe half of what I do if the Lord had not validated things for me by His Spirit. If He had not told me and shown me things about the spirit realm and specific to this writing, about money, I am sure I would be listening to those preachers I followed for many years, doing what they said to do and hoping it was the right thing.

I don't know Mike! You are messing with the tithe! That is

the foundation of what we believe about money. Yes it is. I know people who have faithfully tithed all their lives and still live in lack. Am I saying God is not faithful, that He has not honored His Word? NO! He is faithful! But He does not honor the rules of men and is not compelled or bound to do what we think or say outside of His Word and His instruction. He honors HIS Word.

Let me tell you of a conversation I had with the Lord.

I was at work one day talking to the Lord about many things. I was telling Him thank you for certain things in my life and He was answering me just like you would have a conversation with your Dad. It was so spontaneous and flowing that I didn't even realize what was going on until about five minutes into our conversation. Suddenly it dawned on me to ask the Lord about a prophecy someone had given to me recently and whether this word was from Him. I said

"Lord, will you give me a confirmation that this prophetic word is from you?"

"Yes, I will give you a confirmation." The Lord responded.

So at this point I was silent and listening to hear what he would say next. Often He gives me a scripture that I don't immediately recognize, that will be "spot on" to verify what He has told me. This time however it was different.

"I'll give you a confirmation" the Lord continued, "I'll give you a thousand dollars. How is that for a confirmation?"

By this time in my walk with the Lord I had learned (probably the hard way) that when He says something to me that seems over the top, that I should just say "thank you" or "yes Lord."

"Thank you." I responded. But then He continued.

"You can do whatever you want with this money. All of it is yours and you can spend it any way you like."

Wait a second... Jesus just told me ALL of it was mine and I could spend it all? Doesn't that go against scripture? Why would Jesus tell me something like that? He didn't even tell me "You had better give me my share first!" He said I could have it all. I knew from the gentle way He was speaking to me that this was not some trick from Him. He was answering prayer, blessing me and instructing me just like a good Father would do.

"Thank you Lord. Lord, what do you want me to do?" I asked Him.

He said, "Sow, so that I can give you the greater blessing."

Notice here that he did not say "tithe" on this. He said sow.

*For those of you reading this and thinking that I'm letting people "off the hook" so to speak, you would be wrong. The lessons are far from over.

"OK Lord. What do you want me to do?" I asked Him.

At this point, the Lord told me what He wanted me to do so that He could give me a greater blessing. I didn't even ask what that blessing was so that I could decide if it was worth it. I know His plans are far greater than anything I could ever dream for myself. I could not dream up a blessing that would be greater than what He desired to give to me.

Now unto him that is able to do exceeding abundantly above all that we ask or think, according to the power that worketh in us, (Ephesians 3:20 KJV)

But as it is written, Eye hath not seen, nor ear heard, neither have entered into the heart of man, the things which God hath prepared for them that love him. (1.Corinthians 2:9 KJV)

Our conversation ended with me just amazed at His goodness toward me. I would just watch for His word now to come to pass.

The next day was very normal, nothing out of the ordinary happened and after dinner Gordana and I were relaxing at the breakfast table having coffee. There was a knock at the door and it was a couple we had not seen for quite a while, who said that they had just felt to come and visit with us. We invited them in and had a great time of fellowship. Just as they were about to leave, the man said "Can I talk to you for just a moment?" so we went into another room, as I was anticipating that perhaps he wanted me to pray about something. He took out from his pocket an envelope and gave it to me. "The Lord told me to give this to you" he explained. I believe you know what was in the envelope.

Two weeks later, having obeyed the Lord's instructions, our family received one of the greatest breakthroughs of our lives. That was the greater blessing the Lord had talked to me about.

The Lord taught me many things through this one encounter with him. He gives seed to the sower, He gives direction for our money so that we can receive greater blessing, He does not require every dime He is due, He is a good and loving Father and obedience is better than sacrifice. (1 Samuel 15:22)

One of the things that I believe about the Lord is that He is infinitely more just than we are. If our own children are trying to obey us, whether about money or anything else, and they don't exactly get it right, do we punish them? I do not. I instruct and correct because I want them to "get it." Why would we ever think that God is not as loving as we are? We must stop thinking of ourselves as outsiders looking in, as servants that have a very limited relationship with God. We are sons of God and joint hers with Christ.

Andrew Wommack is one of the most solid and scripturally sound people I know of.

He puts it this way. "A lot of people think that if they don't give the right amount in the right place, God will take it from them through tragedy or illnesses. That sounds more like the Godfather than God the Father. We don't need to be in fear over this issue of our finances."

Where Did We Go Off Course?

A few hundred years after the Lord ascended, we suddenly had government and satan sticking their hands into the "church." Suddenly the government was going to make a place for us, a legitimate recognition of Christianity, however with one little catch... we want to blend other religious practices with it to appease other religious groups. That sounds just like government today and the "government" of the "church" today. Can you imagine first century believers going along with that? People cry today about "crislam" not realizing we have had the influence of mixture for many years.

The "church" stopped being the ecclesia, and took on a different form and life. You can't have a man-made melding of religion and be led of the Spirit at the same time. Now of course I know that there has been a remnant all along. I do understand that but I am speaking specifically on how our understanding has been affected by man's influence in the church.

The next thing you know we are in the Dark Ages where only the select few are deemed worthy to actually understand the scripture and the common folk must rely on their interpretation and honesty and their walk with God to define and shape their own. This was why it was the Dark Ages. Darkness reigned and godless people led the church, charging people for everything from baptism to salvation. Special indulgences were sold, so that those who had not accepted the Lord as their savior could be saved anyway, through loved ones giving money for them to the "church."

The whole "special group" thing is still alive and well today. I am constantly being corrected by leaders in the church who tell me that the things I tell people are for everyone, are in reality only for the select few. Those who are more active in the church and more spiritual than the common believer. An Apostle from Africa recently told me that this is the equivalent of the Modern Dark Ages. I agree with him.

Perversion of the gospel was rampant, and although some of us know all this and do not in any way embrace any of this error, we still have the framework of it working in many of our churches.

Let's Take a Look

First of all, we can just rule out those churches that do not believe or preach the Gospel of Jesus Christ. That is a given. So many of the mainline churches do not believe in sin nor redemption from it. The blood of Jesus means nothing to them. Jesus is neither their savior, their God, King or Lord. We understand this. I'm talking about us and what we are dealing with.

The church mentality is that the pastor or the leaders are in control. Whether you are allowed to play a role in the church is up to certain people in the church. Have you not been allowed yet to pray for the sick? Are there mission trips you would have liked to have been included on? Are you accepted in the little groups within the group or are you still an outsider? This can only happen in the "church." In the Kingdom there are no little special groups where you are excluded. This is all part of the "Only I can hear from God group', that seeks to exercise control.

Last week I had an interesting phone call from a "prophet." He told me "I am a prophet and it has been verified by a very famous prophet! He also told me that you are not a prophet!" You have to obey me because I am the prophet, not you!"

I let him speak much more than I should have and he just continued on, telling me how he was recognized by all these important people, and how important he was. He very angrily told me how I had a much lower and lesser role in God's plan.

I was not in any way bothered by this because I am very grateful and very comfortable in the little job God has given me to do. The Lord knows what makes me happy and fulfilled and I don't need anyone to validate that. I have an audience of one, as I know you have heard it said.

But you see, he needed that validation from the church group, the special people said he was important now. This is the kind of thing that we are dealing with. There is a structure in place that people do not want to challenge, even in their own thoughts.

When it comes to money, I have to be careful that what I am writing is helpful and not just a stern rebuke to those who would not read it anyway. We are told in the church to bring the tithes and offering into the storehouse, right? Who is that storehouse? Is it money given to God for His purpose or do we just give it to the church we belong to and then our responsibility is done. There! We have done our duty! Let's go a little further. What church or ministry even counts? What about a ministry who has no official place to meet, do they count? What about a ministry that is not sanctioned by the government, do they count? Can we give our money to "non-official" ministries and still have God bless us?

Is God more impressed if we send that $100.00 to the guy on

TV with the nice clothes and big organization, than He would be if we gave the money to one of our kids who wants to make sandwiches for homeless people? Would that money given to our kids even count with God? We have been entrained to believe, that the organization and the fact that it is organized or big and impressive, is where God wants our money to go. That is where the blessing is! Give to the structure of the church without question and without hesitation. That is church mentality.

When it comes to money, we always think giving to God means giving the money to someone else. No. It means giving it to God.

The Kingdom

What does the Kingdom look like?

"The kingdom of heaven is like treasure hidden in a field. When a man found it, he hid it again, and then in his joy went and sold all he had and bought that field. (Matthew 13:44 NIV)

For the kingdom of God is not a matter of eating and drinking, but of righteousness, peace and joy in the Holy Spirit, (Romans 14:17 NIV)

The Kingdom is not a matter of having a physical or earthly confirmation. It is not a matter of do this, this and that. When you were born again you became heir of God and it's His good pleasure to give you the Kingdom. You are not just some cog in a machine or in a group, plodding along in your place, but you are a child of the most high God. You are not someone warming a pew who needs validation from anyone but God Himself. It doesn't matter if the rest of the world knows it or understands it, you are a gateway of Heaven and rivers of living water flow from you. You are so far beyond what the human mind can understand, we must have the mind of Christ. Think about that.

The Kingdom of Heaven is at hand is your reality. We are not going to church or to a meeting hoping to get something from God, we have been given all things and are going to release something of God to those around us. The Kingdom is not "let's go see the man or woman of God" as if it were an odd and unusual thing, but rather, we are the man or woman of God also. The Kingdom is not driving all over the earth trying to find someone to pray, but realizing who we are in Christ and moving and speaking from that authority on our own behalf and for others as well. Once we begin to really see who we are everything begins to shift.

When we speak of money, there is no need to find someone more qualified to do God's work, someone "official" that Heaven recognizes. You are that person. Yes, that seems like a weight of responsibility if we reason in the natural. The scripture says that His burden is light and His yoke is easy.

For my yoke is easy, and my burden is light. (Matthew 11:30 KJV)

When you hear someone say "Give your money to the man of God." Your response should be "I am the man (woman) of God. What is the Father saying to do?" When I hear someone preaching, "Bring your tithes into the storehouse," my spirit says that my tithes are already in the storehouse, and have been since they were entrusted to me as a son and steward of God. The only question I must ask is what is my Father saying that I should do?

We have been way too afraid of God in an unholy fear that if we don't do as we have been instructed, our already lackluster financial position will get worse. We must give the Lord more credit than this!

That's one great thing about seeing in the spiritual dimension and allowing God the great blessing of having His angels come and talk to you openly. You can literally see His mercy and grace being given to you. I have been corrected a number of times by the Lord and His angels, and it is always about putting me back on track and not doling out some kind of punishment upon me. That is our God.

So... I have good news... The good news is that we are not under obligation to give God ten percent. However here is the kicker... everything we have belongs to Him. We are stewards as well as His family. When I began to get this revelation, the Lord lifted us out of our mentality that said as long as we gave ten percent, we would be blessed. As heirs of God and administrators of the Kingdom you will quite likely give much, much more! Hey! That's not fair! Ten percent isn't enough?!

Once you make room for God to do the supernatural in your finances things will change. It isn't about you figuring out how to give God more money. In the Kingdom, God gives seed to the sower. It is a supernatural thing!

You remember the testimony that I shared? That has happened many times. The Lord has spoken to myself or my wife Gordana and said "I want you to bless so and so with x amount of money." We do not try to figure out how to make it happen. All we need to do is say "yes Lord." Because it is HIS responsibility to give seed to the sower.

This is another area where people have gone off the rails. I wish I had a nickel for every time I have heard someone say "even if you have to borrow or put it on your credit card, sow now!" This is not scriptural! God says He gives the seed. So what are we doing trying to solve this issue another way?

But Mike what about the lady that went out and borrowed all those containers and pots? Yes she went and borrowed. This is found in Second Kings.

3Then he said, "Go, borrow vessels from everywhere, from all your neighbors—empty vessels; do not gather just a few. 4

And when you have come in, you shall shut the door behind you and your sons; then pour it into all those vessels, and set aside the full ones."

5 So she went from him and shut the door behind her and her sons, who brought the vessels to her; and she poured it out. 6 Now it came to pass, when the vessels were full, that she said to her son, "Bring me another vessel."

And he said to her, "There is not another vessel." So the oil ceased. 7 Then she came and told the man of God. And he said, "Go, sell the oil and pay your debt; and you and your sons live on the rest." (2 Kings 4:3 NKJV)

Notice she is not borrowing oil. She is borrowing vessels to receive the (oil) increase. So on that same line, if you went out and borrowed wallets and purses and strong boxes to receive the blessing and overflow, I guess that would be good.

What I'm trying to convey is that we cannot depend upon others to instruct us as if that absolves us from hearing from God for ourselves. In the Kingdom there is a level of responsibility we take on. The good news about that is that we can have assurance that if we place our money where the Father tells us to, the blessings will come according to His word. Obedience is better than sacrifice!

So two things...

Ask the Lord to Provide Supernaturally

If you want to see supernatural increase in action and God actually supernaturally giving you seed, do this. Ask the Holy Spirit to highlight someone that He wants to bless and tell you who that is. If you are married, ask the Lord also for a confirmation so that you are in agreement. Then tell the Lord this...

"Lord everything that you give us supernaturally this week, we will give to so and so."

If you want to see God provide supernaturally, do this. I will have to tell you though. Many times we say this and we may be thinking fifty dollars or a hundred dollars in our mind. What do you do then when a thousand comes in? It's going to happen. But God does not make this difficult. He will show himself faithful with fifty and give you the opportunity to honor your word. Then He will increase you, then He will increase you again. If he gives you the thousand and you cant quite bring yourself to give it, then He will take you back to the hundred level until you see that you can trust Him.
God gives seed to the sower.

Hear God's Voice for Yourself

Also, if you want to see your seed blessed and multiplied beyond what you have seen and experienced, hearing God's voice is important. Jesus said...

Then answered Jesus and said unto them, Verily, verily, I say unto you, The Son can do nothing of himself, but what he seeth the Father do: for what things soever he doeth, these also doeth the Son likewise. (John 5:19 KJV)

You see, even the Lord Jesus would only do what he saw the Father do. He is not only our Savior and Lord, He is our example and role model. Pattern your life after His no matter what anyone else says and you will be blessed and be walking in God's will.

You may or may not agree with the things I have written here but I will tell you that most people spend more time judging how much money to spend on a cell phone and making sure they make a wise choice, than they do judging where to put the money that God has entrusted to them. I am not throwing rocks at you. This was me for years.

Please just pray about these things. I never ask people to believe apart from the revelation of God. We just have to be willing to hear Him.

4

Popular Teachings

In the area of financial breakthrough and the revelation the Lord has given to me about the resources of Heaven and walking in divine provision, I want to reiterate obedience is better than sacrifice, and tie that truth to a couple other things that the Lord has shown me.

We know there are scriptures that tell us what we should expect. Yes I said expect. If we could not expect God's Word to come to pass, that would be very odd indeed. So we have an expectation, but most people are not seeing the breakthrough. I will give you a little hint about things to come and tell you that supernatural is a key word when you talk about the provision of God. If we have to figure it all out, there is a problem.

Of course I'm not saying we should be ignorant about finances or how to pay bills etc. I'm saying that just as it is in healing or with miracles, there is a level that goes beyond the "normal." That is where we need to be.

But my God shall supply all your need according to his riches in glory by Christ Jesus. (Philippians 4:19 KJV)

I have been young, and now am old; yet have I not seen the righteous forsaken, nor his seed begging bread. (Psalm 37:25 KJV)

When we look at the disconnect between what the Word says and where we are, we can't help but look at and evaluate popular teaching in the church about money. Every time there is a fund drive or a give-a-thon at church or on TV, we see certain teachings that get presented over and over. First, let me say that many of the teachings we know to be true. I often use the example of the message "bake me a cake first" because it is a popular message that most people know. There are many messages and ideas and beliefs that I would ask you to really pray about.

Obedience is Better than Sacrifice

We know this verse. I have known this verse for many years and yet somehow the Lord brings us deeper revelation as we ask and expect it. Can I just say at the risk of offending some people that many times we have ideas or mindsets that sound good but are not God. They are things we have learned along the way that we embrace that are wrong. For example: the idea that poverty brings humility. I named this one because it is an obvious one to most. We have to unlearn those things to come into alignment with His Word.

There is a way which seemeth right unto a man, but the end thereof are the ways of death. (Proverbs 14:12 KJV)

There are many, many areas where we need to come into alignment with God's economy, if we are to see the breakthrough. I want you to prayerfully consider this one.

The Size of the Seed

Again, I don't want to lead you through scriptures that you already know. You are mature believers and I know that. Just think of the verses you know about seed and sowing and also what you have heard people teach, and consider what the Lord showed me one day as I sat in a meeting and watched an offering being taken.

The Word Given

Up until the time of the offering, the anointing was not only present but tangibly real. I was undeniably blessed. When the time for the offering came, the speaker felt the need to call people to plant thousand dollar seeds. As a matter of fact, that was the only number he mentioned. He spoke about the thousand dollar seed and increase he had seen. He told testimonies about the thousand dollar seed and although I believe in planting such seeds, something just was not right.

The Lord Spoke to Me

The Lord spoke to me as this was happening. "What do you think of this?" the Lord asked me. I told the Lord that I believe in planting large seeds. The Lord reminded me of a time once that I had heard a minister say, "There's something about a thousand dollar seed that moves God's hand." "Do you believe that?" the Lord asked. I told the Lord that I don't believe that and the scripture that talks about the widow's mite, makes that very clear.

Jesus sat down opposite the place where the offerings were put and watched the crowd putting their money into the temple treasury. Many rich people threw in large amounts. 42 But a poor widow came and put in two very small copper coins, worth only a few cents.43 Calling his disciples to him, Jesus said, "Truly I tell you, this poor widow has put more into the treasury than all the others. 44 They all gave out of their wealth; but she, out of her poverty, put in everything— all she had to live on." (Mark 12:41-44 NIV)

As the teaching of the thousand dollar seed was being presented, the Lord told me to look around the room. As someone who also sees in the spirit, I knew the Lord was telling me to look in that dimension. As I looked, I saw a very subtle spirit of despair and disappointment come upon many, many people. It was heart-breaking to see. The Lord told me. "Do you see that elderly woman? She has fifteen dollars with her that she was so excited to be able to sow tonight." I looked at the woman. You didn't have to be a seer to see the discouragement on her face. "Look at that boy" the Lord told me. "He has his allowance with him that he was going to sow. He will not go up and give it now, because He thinks it doesn't matter. He is being taught to believe that I will not honor his two mites."

We know that obedience is better than sacrifice. We have to trust God that He will not withhold the blessing as we are willfully and truthfully trying to yield to His voice and follow His will where our money is concerned.

The Little Seeds

Those who know me, know that I am all about the practical things we can actually do pertaining to taking steps of faith to see His will manifested in our lives.

So what about little seeds? I'm saying don't hesitate and don't be ashamed to sow little seeds! One of the most touching things that happened to me recently was after a service, an elderly woman came up to me and tearfully pressed five dollars into my hand because she wanted to bless me. Do you how much that meant to me?

Yes, we also sow large seeds and sometimes it stretches our faith to do so, but we follow the voice of the Holy Spirit. The Lord told me once to sow a thousand (so you know I'm ok with that amount) Several times He has led us to sow even more. Once the Lord told us to give someone $265.00 to fix their car and as random an amount as that seems, the people called later and mentioned in conversation that they needed $250. for a car repair. Yes we do sow big seeds as well but hear my heart. If all you have, or if all God is telling you is to sow a small seed, He has a reason and if you do He will bless you!

For those of you who receive seed from people, whether big or small, honor it and the people who give it the way the Lord does!

Follow the Spirit

If we follow the voice of the spirit, the amount of seed we give won't always make sense to us. If we reason in the natural, we might say "I'm almost embarrassed to give five or ten dollars. What kind of dent would that even make?" That ten dollars added with the tens or eights or twenties from others, just paid that ministry's bills for the month.

After a service, you might be prompted to go up and slip your three dollars into the speakers pocket but hesitate because you reason "what is three dollars?" When the Lord knows that your three dollars will buy a nice coffee or cold drink for the speaker to enjoy on the way home.

We must listen to the voice of the Spirit and no other. Obedience is better than sacrifice. There are a thousand different scenarios and many of you have lived them. Your "small seed" might just be the answer to someone's prayers.

What about the Third World?

After the Lord spoke to me about the size of someone's seed, I began to think of all the scenarios where this could be applied. I thought about recent trips to certain nations where people are living on a couple of dollars a day. If this teaching of giving a certain large amount to "move God's hand" is true, will God give all these believers each a thousand dollars so that they can also have this blessing? Or is this blessing only for believers in the west?

There was something so compelling and sincere about the way the man presented this teaching, that I must confess the first few times I listened, I sowed the big seeds.

"There's something about a thousand dollar seed that moves the hand of God."

You may want to really pray about that one. So does the Lord honor big amounts more than small? What about five hundred or three hundred or five thousand? I think that we get the idea. I don't care how many scriptures someone uses to prop up this message, it is not true.

Does God honor sacrifice? Of course He does! That fifty dollars you gave to the Pastor or to the building fund that caused you to have to eat light for a couple weeks, God sees and honors. Or the twenty you were saving to go to a movie that you decided to give to the youth mission program, God honors that sacrifice. But God is not impressed with amounts. Those messages have no credibility anywhere except in nations like the U.S.

The Big Seeds

Little seeds or big seeds are all relative to each person. I believe in sowing big seeds and small seeds. I like to sow big seeds. To be perfectly candid with you we have sown lots of those big seeds and small ones as well. We have made sacrifices to give to things that we believe in and it is a blessing to do so. Sow big seeds but do it at the direction of the Lord.

Another popular idea is…

Obey the Man of God

This is another instruction that further emphasizes that divide between the people in ministry and the "regular" people. When a prophet or someone in authority tells you this is the time to give or this is what you should give, it is hard sometimes not to comply. We have this idea reinforced in our church culture, that these are the ones in authority who can speak for God, so they must have heard from Him.

Sometimes this is true and sometimes not.

The Lord reinforced to me the necessity of hearing His voice for myself several times one year.

How to See in the Spirit

Many of you may know that a few years ago at the Lord's direction I wrote a book called How to See in the Spirit. Due to no effort of my own, the book was very well received and the Lord made the book do very well. As you can imagine, people have strange ideas sometimes of what "Christian bestseller" means financially. During one year, I had three confirmations from the Lord that we must learn to hear His voice for ourselves.

One day I got a "nice" phone call from someone in a position of authority in a denomination who decided to remind me in very stern tones, that all the money I was making now belongs to the Lord and His work. This person was implying that I was not giving the Lord His portion. Yes, all my money is the Lord's. I am a steward and even the money I make in other ways such as fixing equipment at work belongs to Him in my perspective. I am quite fine with that.

Then... I had a prophet prophesy that I had never paid tithes on my book income and that the Lord was saying that I should give that money to him (the prophet). I don't want to share so openly about my giving, but I will say that he was so far off the mark it wasn't funny.

Then, I guess to make sure I got the point, the Lord allowed it to happen once again and another prophet also prophesied that I had not given the Lord any money from my books and that I was supposed to give him (the prophet) the money along with a penalty!

In my situation, I knew that none of them were hearing from God because I knew the details of my own finances. But what about when we get an instruction to give that is a bit more vague? This is why we need to hear from the Lord for ourselves.

Confirmations

Yes, there have been times where someone has asked me to give and I felt it was God. God gives confirmations. We can't be wise about everything else and then give money or sow, haphazardly. That would not be good stewardship.

Where no counsel is, the people fall: but in the multitude of counsellers there is safety. (Proverbs 11:14 KJV)

Then the disciples went out and preached everywhere, and the Lord worked with them and confirmed his word by the signs that accompanied it. (Mark 16:20 NIV)

If the Word is from God He will confirm it. I have said it before but it bears repeating. "Biblical faith is not blind faith."

On the topic of giving because the man of God said so, how about the idea of giving to the man of God? We have all heard the scripture about receiving a prophet, and also the famous story of honoring the prophet by making him a cake first, but is everyone that gives that message a man (or woman) of God? Even if they are, are they hearing from God in that moment? And finally, does it matter? I promise I will show you the importance of all this. Sometimes we can look at circumstances in the natural and think it doesn't matter so much, but because of the spiritual implications is does.

God will speak so clearly to you it will be unbelievable. He wants us to hear His voice. His Word says...

My sheep hear my voice, and I know them, and they follow me: (John 10:27 KJV)

Don't be afraid to take the time to sow wisely. I know what I talked about earlier was hard. Many want to make sure they are doing right by the Lord and are doing it with good motives and a clear conscience. They consider it good stewardship, so as I have stated previously, I am not throwing rocks at anybody who is tithing. Tithing is a good way to make it easy to make sure God is in your finances. It is a structure to use. You cannot do these things by rote however. Where I am trying to take you to, is some place where miracles start to happen. Many times the known and comfortable change slowly. We have to make room for that. If we are going to do those things, we should have scripture to back it up, and also an understanding of that scripture in context. The Lord expects us to walk in the light that we have and He is the supplier of that light. Taking someone's word for what God really means is not an option as we seek to walk in supernatural provision. We can't do anything blindly hoping it is correct. In the matter of money, we must understand something has been off with most of us and needs to be fixed.

Delayed Obedience is Disobedience

This is a teaching I have heard many times, especially on the television during fund drives. The hardest thing about coming to understand some of these teachings is that there is a truth to them. Just like there is a truth in the story of the widow who makes the prophet a cake, there is truth in this instruction.

The problem lays in the fact that there must be clarity for us to move. If you truly are hearing the voice of God, and you know that you are hearing Him, yet still don't want to do what He is telling you to do, there is a deeper issue at work that you need to deal with. That is not what is happening with most of the people I know, who are looking for God's blessing and provision. We are not looking for ways to get out of supporting the Gospel or looking for technicalities to get out of giving like some Pharisee. We are living sacrifices to God believing for the manifestation of His promises.

Yes, delayed obedience is disobedience when we clearly hear from God. In today's world, this instruction has become almost a "catch-phrase" during messages about giving or at offering time. We don't need to be convinced to give to God, right? If we are not certain we are hearing God's voice, then delay is not disobedience it is WISDOM. We want to do what the Lord is telling us to do. It does matter.

I have been in many services where I would not really hear the Lord saying to give, yet when the instruction to give was given, I would do it anyway. That seems harmless enough on the surface. I had an extra twenty in my pocket for coffee for the week, but I can do without so much coffee. But many times God had other plans for that money and I had already given it away of my own volition. It is not disobedience to wait for God's voice.

It's a Seed, Not a Harvest

Another popular teaching that I have heard is that if the amount of money God has given you is not all you would ever want, that means it's a seed and not a harvest. On the surface, this teaching sounds wise and if it is presented with conviction, it's hard not to believe it.

I watched as the man of God looked sincerely into the camera and said

"Why are you holding on to that five hundred dollars? Is that the size of the blessing you have been dreaming about? You can't hardly make a car payment with that! If it's not your harvest, it's your seed."

The problem with a teaching like this is that it makes no room for smaller miracles to be miracles. Unless someone just received a million dollars out of the blue, they would possibly never have a harvest their entire lives but only seed.

Judging the amounts according to the previous criteria, would a thousand be a harvest? No. How about fifty thousand? No, that isn't all we would ever want or need. We think about paying off the house or putting the kids through school and realize fifty thousand wouldn't get the job done.
In the scripture it says...

"Whoever can be trusted with very little can also be trusted with much, and whoever is dishonest with very little will also be dishonest with much. (Luke 16:10 NIV)

As a good Father does, the Lord teaches us faithfulness and obedience. He trains us and raises us up, and as we learn how to be faithful with little, the Lord gives us greater. Therefore, when we feel led of the Spirit to sow twenty dollars to the missionary speaking at our church, believing God that the five hundred we need for rent will be supplied, then the five hundred would be a harvest. You could go as low in the amount as you like. Really? Can a hundred be a harvest? How about fifty? Or twenty? There are people across the Earth who if the Lord gave them ten dollars, would gather the family together and worship and praise His name with tears of rejoicing for such a glorious blessing! That is the reality.

Though he were a Son, yet learned he obedience by the things which he suffered; (Hebrews 5:8 KJV)

The reason I share about this teaching is because many people have bank accounts with a little money in them and wonder if they should keep it or sow it. If you hear a teaching such as this, you might be inclined to send it in, when the Lord could be asking you to keep it for another reason, even that of paying bills etc. Again we come back to hearing God's voice and obeying His voice.

Sow While the Spirit is Moving

I was watching a television show recently and the man

speaking was sharing a powerful and uplifting message. As he spoke the message became more intense and his words more passionate until it all led to a crescendo of "it's time to sow NOW".

Now to be honest, when he said something about the spirit moving, I was feeling the presence of the Holy Spirit as he gave his message. It was genuine. When the message shifted, there was a moment of confusion. Where did that anointing go? Why do I not feel it now? Is the enemy trying to derail my blessing? The confusion was only momentary. I knew he was speaking by another spirit when he began to ask for people to sow. I have seen it before in the spirit. (what it looks like)

I was at a service once and just as the pastor was about to talk about the offering, a spirit came across the platform and whispered in his ear. It happens.

The real tragedy is, that there is a spiritual truth here that gets a bad rap. The reality is that when the Spirit is moving, we feel to go forward for prayer or repentance or to sow by the Spirit. If we are led by the Spirit and we sow in these times, it is powerful.

This is similar to being at a meeting where the Glory of God falls in the meeting and miracles just happen. You feel the presence of God so you move in faith because you recognize what is happening. No one has to convince you and there is no confusion, doubt or turmoil. In times like this you can sow by faith and it feels right. There is an inner witness that bears witness with your spirit.

In any movement of God you can see the work of the Spirit, the flesh and the devil. We have to discern which is which. For those of you who have sown during emotional times in meetings, and not seen that harvest that was talked about, this could be why.

On and On it Goes...

There are many teachings, messages and instructions we hear about money and finances and many times we listen because we need that elusive breakthrough. Where did we miss it? As I pointed out, and I pray you get this, many of the messages delivered in the flesh, carry a seed of truth. That is why they can seem so compelling. Also, we need to keep in mind that there are real and true servants of God who can and do prophesy increase or can tell you what the Lord is saying concerning finances. The real issue here is hearing God's voice and knowing His will.

We have to realize that not just for our benefit now but also for the days ahead, we have to learn to be really good stewards and be responsible for the money the Lord entrusts to us. It's not enough to say "I gave my obligation is done." I believe that you agree.

Why it matters so Much

Many will think that I'm making a mountain out of a molehill. Does it really matter so much? All this awareness about every nickel, like we can't make a mistake? No. there is grace for those who are seeking to do God's will and even an amount of grace for those who don't want to think about changing their structure around their money and giving. Why does it matter if we sow into something of the flesh?

Herein lays the problem... If we allow an open door to the enemy to afflict our finances it does not end well for us. That is why every little thing matters. I often tell people when they are seeking the deeper things of the Spirit and the spiritual dimension, to be careful what movies they watch or bring into their homes. Many argue... There was only one bad scene... there were only a few curse words...etc. etc. People say, "I can watch this and it doesn't affect me. It doesn't cause me to want to sin or to want to curse or take the Lord's name in vain." Well, that's great, but you still have opened a door to the enemy into your life and home and possibly your family. It matters. It all matters.

Opening Doors to Your Finances

If you are in a meeting and you feel that you should not give in the offering but someone pressures you to give, that could be a spirit of manipulation. We might think that a few dollars won't matter... I'll get up and go to the front like everyone else and be done with it. In situations like this I would counsel you to not give a nickel. When you take a step of action, sowing into something that doesn't feel right you open a door to that spirit in your finances. I am not saying to be in fear but to only do what you see the Father do.

I recently read something from a friend who said that during the offering the pastor said "Don't hold onto that money! You don't need to go out to eat after the service! Give that money to God."

Here again, what is the Father saying? If you promised your kids you were going out to eat after the service, then you had better show them that as someone who represents Christ, you are someone of your word. If you feel that a sacrifice should be made, then you go without, not them. In every situation I mentioned, we have an opportunity to either hear God's voice or blindly obey an instruction. If we hear, we know we are walking according to His will. If we don't hear, we could be opening doors to the enemy or simply giving money away that the Lord may have given us for another purpose. That is why so many people walk in lack that have sown, and sown, and sown.

We can't be unaware about these things and expect to walk in victory.

I have said some hard things here. I have definitely stepped on some toes. As people who walk in the spirit, we have to see everything from Heaven's perspective. That is what causes us to walk in victory and in supernatural provision.

5

Wisdom Concerning Spiritual Things

There is a price to be paid, make no mistake about that. No matter what you pursue in life, if you desire to obtain something you pay a price. Let me just say at this point that I know Jesus paid it all. Jesus paid the ultimate price. Everything good we have is from Him from our health to our finances. We are not "earning" anything in that respect.

Every good gift and every perfect gift is from above, and comes down from the Father of lights, with whom there is no variation or shadow of turning. (James 1:17 NKJV)

Maybe a better way to say it just to avoid confusion is that there is a choice to be made. Do we choose to think about heavenly things or worldly things? Do we choose to fellowship with the saints or sleep in? Do we choose to study the word or watch that new crime drama? Are we going to pray today or are we going to take a break from prayer? I made the point about paying a price because we are talking about money and kingdom finances and provision in the bigger picture. We often speak of "spending" our time don't we? Whether we are talking about time or money, are we good stewards? Does it really matter where our time or money goes as long as we are giving to God? I believe it does. Being a good steward doesn't mean just giving your share. I don't believe in mindless giving. Jesus said I only do what I see the Father do. That is very specific.

I have heard many people say "It doesn't matter what they do with the money. That's not my business. I gave my ten percent and did my part so the rest is on them." Have you heard that before? I have. I'm reminded of the wicked servant who buried the money entrusted to him.

14 For the kingdom of heaven is like a man traveling to a far country, who called his own servants and delivered his goods to them. 15 And to one he gave five talents, to another two, and to another one, to each according to his own ability; and immediately he went on a journey. 16 Then he who had received the five talents went and traded with them, and made another five talents. 17 And likewise he who had received two gained two more also. 18 But he who had received one went and dug in the ground, and hid his lord's money. 19 After a long time the lord of those servants came and settled accounts with them.

20 "So he who had received five talents came and brought five other talents, saying, 'Lord, you delivered to me five talents; look, I have gained five more talents besides them.' 21 His lord said to him, 'Well done, good and faithful servant; you were faithful over a few things, I will make you ruler over many things. Enter into the joy of your lord.' 22 He also who had received two talents came and said, 'Lord, you delivered to me two talents; look, I have gained two more talents besides them.' 23 His lord said to him, 'Well done, good and faithful servant; you have been faithful over a few things, I will make you ruler over many things. Enter into the joy of your lord.'

24 "Then he who had received the one talent came and said, 'Lord, I knew you to be a hard man, reaping where you have not sown, and gathering where you have not scattered seed. 25 And I was afraid, and went and hid your talent in the ground. Look, there you have what is yours.'

26 "But his lord answered and said to him, 'You wicked and lazy servant, you knew that I reap where I have not sown,

and gather where I have not scattered seed. 27 So you ought to have deposited my money with the bankers, and at my coming I would have received back my own with interest. 28 Therefore take the talent from him, and give it to him who has ten talents.

29 'For to everyone who has, more will be given, and he will have abundance; but from him who does not have, even what he has will be taken away. 30 And cast the unprofitable servant into the outer darkness. There will be weeping and gnashing of teeth.'

What do you take from this scripture? The wicked servant did not put his master's money where it would bring increase. Is it really ok to give without thought of what the master's money yields? No. We are responsible for the things that are entrusted to us. We cannot shift the responsibility onto someone else. "Well... Pastor so and so told me to. It's his fault." No, it isn't. Wisdom in all things. Where am I going?

Merchandising the Anointing for $1000

Not long ago I spoke in a church where there were a lot of people who desired to be used of God in ministry. To be fair, that could be said about a lot of the churches I where I have spoken. But after one of the meetings a young man approached me and asked for a moment of my time. I knew by the spirit that he was serious about the things of God. The Lord told me to speak with him. He told me he had an important decision to make the next day and he asked if I could either give him direction or pray concerning his decision.

Then he told me the situation. This young man had approached a well-known apostle and asked for a prayer of impartation so that he could be used of the Lord in greater measure. I myself have stood in the prayer lines of people I admire, so I could relate to this. The apostle told him that he would release his anointing to the young man and be his "covering" if the young man would pay him $1,000. He was taken a bit by surprise he said, but didn't want to miss out if this was God. But on the other hand a $1,000 is a lot of money so he wanted to be sure. His question to me was "Should I pay this money so that he will pray for me and be my covering?" The apostle was coming to attend the meeting the next day so he had to have an answer before then.

I laid my hand on his shoulder and closed my eyes to pray but before I could even start, the Lord spoke to me. "Explain to him the basics concerning apostles and prophets. I knew what the Lord was telling me. I opened my eyes after my five-second "prayer" and explained a few things to him about apostles and prophets.

I told him that apostles and prophets are foundational offices in the body of Christ. They are they ones that allow others to build upon them. They are the ones that build you up, equip you, prepare you, and launch you by the Spirit of God. I explained that if an apostle feels led of the Lord to be your covering, it is a very serious thing. It is not something that is done lightly but is a responsibility before God. I told him that I myself have been asked to be someone's covering but would not do it unless the Lord told me to do so. It's serious.

I explained that one of the marks of the apostles and prophets of God is humility. Not just gifting but humility and Christ-like character. There is no job beneath them because they are the low place... the foundation. A servant is not above his master. An apostle will wash your feet. An apostle is the ultimate servant with the heart of a servant. Think Jesus. An apostle delights in blessing those whom the Lord has given to him. An apostle will pray for you and bless you.
He said he witnessed to the things I had said and had decided not to pay the money for the anointing.

What Does the Scripture Say?

Maybe the apostle was trying to test the young man's heart. Maybe... But that wasn't what God revealed to me. Jesus told the rich young ruler to sell all he had and give the money to the poor and then follow Him.

21 Jesus said unto him, If thou wilt be perfect, go and sell that thou hast, and give to the poor, and thou shalt have treasure in heaven: and come and follow me.

22 But when the young man heard that saying, he went away sorrowful: for he had great possessions. (Matthew 19:21-22 KJV)

Jesus did not say "Sell all you have and give me the money." No, the bible says to avoid even the appearance of evil. (1 Thessalonians 5:22)

I'm reminded of the story of Simon the sorcerer who wished to purchase the power that the disciples carried.

18 And when Simon saw that through the laying on of the apostles' hands the Holy Spirit was given, he offered them money, 19 saying, "Give me this power also, that anyone on whom I lay hands may receive the Holy Spirit."

20 But Peter said to him, "Your money perish with you, because you thought that the gift of God could be purchased with money! (Acts 18:18-20 NKJV)

The young man I spoke to was not a "Simon" by any stretch of the imagination but rather just a young man who was hungry for God and did not want to miss out on an opportunity from God. The Lord showed me that He was going to use the young man mightily in the days ahead. I'm excited for him.

The Role of Money in the Kingdom

Again, we must be wise and responsible with that which God entrusts to us. Whether we are talking about $1,000 or $10 we have to realize that it all matters. Do you want to see the blessing of God upon your life? Realize every financial decision, every seed sown and dollar given has an impact one way or the other.... For you or against you.

Yes, we bless people. We love to bless the apostles and prophets. We are part of a plan and if we want to walk in kingdom abundance, we must see that nothing is haphazard. We must be good and faithful stewards putting the Lord's money where He instructs us to so that it will bear great fruit.

Aligning With the Right People

This topic is something that affects so many in the body of Christ. From all the examples that I have given so far over the course of this short book, you can see that there are both people who are misguided in ministry, self-serving or even completely dishonest. Those are the facts. Please don't kill the messenger. We as believers tend to believe the best about everyone. That isn't necessarily a bad thing, but that kindness must be tempered by wisdom.

So many today follow the church business model of coming up with programs and promotions to bring in the money God needs. To many this is right. We do have to do our part... even Paul made tents to support himself in the gospel, but there is a difference between taking steps of faith and manipulation. We have to align with those whose lives and ministries honor the Lord so that our "talents" are bringing increase and we are not just throwing them in a hole.

6

Setting Things Right

I know that I've said some things that may challenge you. As I mentioned earlier, pray about these things. If there wasn't an issue of some kind you probably wouldn't be reading this book. Let's start taking this as seriously as we would the illness of someone we love. Many people's finances are "sick." You've heard it said that the definition of insanity is "doing the same thing over and over and expecting a different result." Let's cry out for some real godly wisdom on this topic.

Repent

Repent? Really? All the things that we have done of a questionable nature with our money, we need to repent for those things. Go back through your memories and ask the Holy Spirit to help you. Every incident where you felt strange about giving... every time you gave and knew you shouldn't have... every time you were manipulated into giving... every time you threw money away foolishly... every time you spent money on ungodly things... repent of those things. You know the definition of repent is to turn away and go the opposite direction. This is too important to miss.

A Prayer of Repentance

Father in Heaven, Please forgive me of every offense and every sin concerning money. Forgive me to yielding to or opening any door to manipulation or influence of the enemy into my life, home and finances. Cleanse me now from all unrighteousness according to your word. I repent of any action that has offended you in any way or has been dishonoring to you. Lord cleanse us now. Father I also declare on the authority of the word that every door that was opened to the enemy is now closed. I declare that every ungodly tie or connection of any sort is also now broken. I thank you for your forgiveness and restoration of this part of my life. In Jesus' name. Amen.

Moving in the Right Direction

It took me some considerable time before I was moving in the right direction concerning my finances and really in wisdom in general in regard to spiritual things. One of the biggest impacts for me was when the Lord opened up more fully the spiritual realm to me. It cleared up a lot of confusion I had on many things.

I think back to some of the messages that I had sown into and I would cry if I didn't know that God has redeemed the time and resources for me. Many thousands of dollars passed from my hands before I understood that I couldn't take things on face value, I had to have a confirmation from the Spirit of God. I think back to all the "testimonies" that I have heard about Rolex watches, custom sports cars and designer clothes, and I don't want to admit that I was that immature to think that those things validated a person's message about sowing.

Once I repented for blindly going along the wide path, our lives took on a new dynamic of blessing. Multiple miracles of blessings and supernatural blessings. There were dreams that facilitated blessings and supernatural seeds that came that brought blessings. Those are some of the things that I will share in book two of this message. I pray that the things that I have shared thus far have resonated with you. That the Holy Spirit will reveal things to you in the coming season so that this type of ongoing blessing is also a part of your life.

A Prayer of Blessing

Father in Heaven, I pray your richest blessing upon the person reading this prayer. I pray that wisdom and revelation come and manifest their presence in their lives. Father, let the mind of Christ be established in them so that they think and reason by the power of the Holy Spirit. I declare blessings upon the minds, bodies, souls and spirits. I declare the blessings of God upon their health and well-being, their thoughts, dreams and emotions, their lives, families and homes. Father let their wallets, purses and bank accounts be blessed with supernatural financial increase. Let their businesses, work and income prosper beyond anything that they have ever known. Let the angels of the Lord fight for them and bring to pass the Father's good will in their lives. Set a hedge of protection over them and their families and keep them in the palm of your hand. Teach them about supernatural provision that you have provided for your children and give them the grace to walk in it. In Jesus' name. Amen.

About Book Two...

Book two of supernatural provision will share many testimonies of miracles of blessings as well as financial miracles. I will share about things like prayer, prophetic gestures, obedience to the word, finding/receiving seed, sacrificial giving, honoring the things you want in your life and much more.

If you have been offended by the things I have shared in this book, I'm sorry. If the things I have said have resonated with you then I would encourage you to also read book two of this message.

Thank you.
Michael

OTHER BOOKS BY THIS AUTHOR
(Available at Amazon)

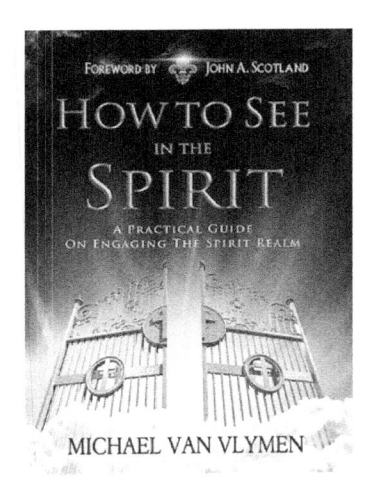

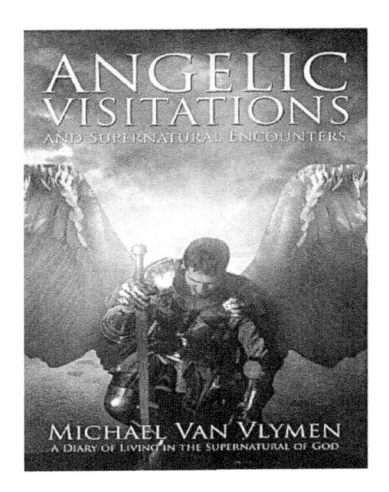

At Amazon.com or your favorite book seller.

About the Author

Michael Van Vlymen is an author and speaker who teaches about the supernatural things of God. It's Michael's passion to share that everyone can learn to see in the spirit realm and walk in the supernatural. Michael travels the world sharing and teaching the revelation God has given him and equipping Believers to fulfill their destiny in Christ. Michael is the author of several books including "How to See in the Spirit" a best-seller on the subject of spiritual sight.